PREDESTINATION

"...TO BE CONFORMED TO THE

IMAGE OF HIS SON"

LESLIE M. JOHN

PREDESTINATION

"...TO BE CONFORMED TO THE

IMAGE OF HIS SON"

LESLIE JOHN

All scriptures in electronic format are taken from KJV and Darby Translation by Public Domain, and

- New International Version (NIV)
- Holy Bible, New International Version®, NIV® Copyright © 1973, 1978, 1984, 2011 by Biblica, Inc.® Used by permission. All rights reserved worldwide.
- English Standard Version (ESV)
- The Holy Bible, English Standard Version Copyright © 2001 by Crossway Bibles, a division of Good News Publishers.

Description:

The exposition that I present here is as I understand, and as revealed to me by the Holy Spirit, rather than following the very familiar and conflicting interpretations of:

1. Total Depravity
2. Unconditional Election
3. Limited Atonement
4. Irresistible Grace
5. Perseverance of Saints

"Predestination" is a biblical doctrine and if it is understood correctly our hope in Lord Jesus Christ and in our eternity increases, thus honoring God for loving us. Much of the problem of understanding "Predestination" comes from the fact that believers tend to have one sided view of the doctrine as taught in one's childhood, or in early stages of one's Christian life. First of all it should be understood that "Predestination" emphasizes on the end result than that of intermediate stages.

Predestination is a doctrine of God marking out the believers in Christ to conform to the image of His Son. However, we cannot skip meditating on Salvation because only those who are saved will be conformed to the image of His Son.

Our gratitude towards God increases when we understand that God did not predestinate some to destruction, and some to salvation, but He predestinated sons adopted by Him to be conformed to the image of His Son, Lord Jesus Christ.

ISBN-13:978-0-9882933-0-4
ISBN-10: 0-9882933-0-7

Contents

CHAPTER 1 DEPRAVITY

"Predestination" is a very vigorously debated topic for many years now. The exposition that I present here is as I understand, and as revealed to me by the Holy Spirit, rather than following the very familiar and conflicting interpretations of:

1. Total Depravity
2. Unconditional Election
3. Limited Atonement
4. Irresistible Grace
5. Perseverance of Saints

"Predestination" is a biblical doctrine and if it is understood correctly our hope in Lord Jesus Christ and in our eternity increases, thus honoring God for loving us.

Much of the problem of understanding "Predestination" comes from the fact that believers tend to have one sided view of the doctrine as taught in one's childhood, or in early stages of one's Christian life.

First of all it should be understood that "Predestination" emphasizes on the end result than that of intermediate stages.

Predestination is a doctrine of God marking out the believers in Christ to conform to the image of His Son. However, we cannot skip meditating on Salvation because only those who are saved will be conformed to the image of His Son.

Our gratitude towards God increases when we understand that God did not predestinate some to destruction, and some to salvation, but He predestinated sons adopted by Him to be conformed to the image of His Son, Lord Jesus Christ.

JESUS SAID "Except a man be born again, he cannot see the kingdom of God"

What does it mean to be born-again?

"Jesus answered and said unto him, Verily, verily, I say unto thee, Except a man be born again, he cannot see the kingdom of God. Nicodemus saith unto him, How can a man be born when he is old? can he enter the second time into his mother's womb, and be born? Jesus answered, Verily, verily, I say unto thee, Except a man be born of water and of the Spirit, he cannot enter into the kingdom of God". (John 3:3-5)

Jesus Christ died for our sins; he rose from the dead and ascended into heaven. He is now seated at the right hand of the Majesty and He is coming again soon.

THIS IS HOW SIN CONQUERED MAN

This is where the first depravity is seen. Holy Bible says God created man in his own image. God planted a garden eastward in Eden and he put there the man whom God called Adam. The garden was indeed beautiful with every tree pleasant to sight and good for food.

The LORD God made every tree to grow from the ground, the tree of life also in the midst of the garden, and the tree of knowledge of good and evil. The LORD God put the man into the Garden of Eden to dress it and keep it. He said to the man that he may freely eat of every tree of the garden but of the tree of knowledge of good and evil he shall not eat; and in the day he eats it he shall surely die. God saw that man was alone and the LORD God said that the man should not be alone.

God decided to give a "help meet" for man. The LORD God caused a deep sleep upon Adam and while he was sleeping God took one of the ribs of the man and made a woman out of the rib and brought to him. Adam called her as "Woman" because she was taken out of Man.

God said to the man to be fruitful, multiply, replenish the earth, and subdue it and have dominion over the fish of the sea, fowl of the air and every living thing that moves on the earth. (Genesis 2:8-28).

THIS IS HOW SATAN DECEIVED MAN

The serpent, which was more subtle than any other beast of the field, deceived the woman with his enticing words. The serpent spoke to her and convinced her that God did not tell the truth.

The woman yielded to the temptation of the serpent. She saw that the tree was good for food and pleasure for the eyes and thought the tree would give her intelligence. She took of its fruit and ate and also gave to her husband and he ate it.

The eyes of both of them opened and they knew that they were naked.

They made aprons for themselves with fig-leaves and when they heard the voice of God, whose name is "Jehovah Elohim" they hid themselves from his presence. The first man had the choice to choose good or evil for him, but he chose evil.

Jehovah Elohim called man and asked him where he was? The man said he feared because he was naked and hid himself.

God demanded an answer from the man as to who said to him that he was naked and questioned if he had he eaten fruit of the tree that he was asked not to eat from! The man blamed woman and the woman blamed the serpent.

CHAPTER 2 SOVEREIGN GOD

Careful reading of Romans Chapter 9 reveals God's dealing with the children of Israel. Apostle Paul was a Jew and belonged to the tribe of Benjamin (Philippians 3:5). He expresses his concern for the children of Israel.

The first five verses speak of his continual sorrow in his heart for them because they rejected Jesus Christ as their Messiah. He wishes that he could be accursed if his brethren and kinsmen, to whom belonged the adoption, the glory and the covenants and the giving of the Law, accepted Jesus Christ as their Savior.

In discussions about Predestination and Freewill often there is a tendency to say first of all, predestination is all about salvation, while the truth is that it is all about conforming to the image of Lord Jesus Christ and secondly compare —

- JACOB OVER ESAU
- VESSELS OF WRATH AND MERCY
- PHARAOH'S HEART

Apostle Paul narrates about God's choice of Jacob over Esau and how they struggled with each other even when they were in the womb of Rebecca. God chose Jacob over Esau and blessed him.

Jacob became father of the twelve tribes. God renamed Jacob as "Israel" and called the children of Israel as "My People".

Therefore my people shall know my name: therefore they shall know in that day that I am he that doth speak: behold, it is I. (Isaiah 52:6)

Can anyone question God's actions? No. God said that He will have mercy and compassion on whom He decides to have compassion.

"For he saith to Moses, I will have mercy on whom I will have mercy, and I will have compassion on whom I will have compassion" (Romans 9:15)

This verse is grossly misinterpreted that God has arbitrarily chose Jacob over Esau and rendered Esau and all others as vessels of wrath. God choose Jacob in His mercy and blessed Him but that does not mean He has decided to treat all others in His wrath or predestinated them for Hell. Can a vessel say to the potter as to why the potter made it vessel unto honor and the other for dishonor?

"Hath not the potter power over the clay, of the same lump to make one vessel unto honour, and another unto dishonour?" (Romans 9:21)

Vessels of wrath were not marked out or selected before the foundation of the world, but the vessels of mercy were marked out before the foundation to be conformed to the image of Lord Jesus Christ.

Everyone has the opportunity to come to the Lord and accept Him as the Savior and have everlasting life. God has the power to make His own decision whom to choose for bestowing His blessings upon them. As Paul writes who can find fault with God and who can resist His will?

God raised Pharaoh that His glory may be manifest but at the same time God cannot be held guilty of Pharaoh's hardening of heart. Close look at few verses reveal that God hardened Pharaoh's heart after Pharaoh hardened his heart.

God made firm the hardening of heart by Pharaoh because Pharaoh, as evil as he was, harassed the children of Israel and hardened his heart against them. In Romans Chapter 1 also similar theme is seen.

When man hardens his heart and chooses to be in sin God allows him to harden his heart more and hands him over to his sin.

Every sin has consequences and man is responsible for the consequences that follow after committing sin. Many diseases in man are the result of sin and the consequences of sin become like stench in the nostrils of man ever trying to get rid of them.

Example is seen in one of the plagues that was removed by God as Moses prayed to the Lord based on Pharaoh's request frogs died but the heaps of frogs were still left behind for Pharaoh's people to gather them and the land stank.

This is how sin leaves behind in a man something that reminds it. However, we should be glad the Lord does not remember our sins that are pardoned. (Exodus 8:13-14, Hebrews 14:10-17)

The phrase "I will harden his heart" used by God occurs in Exodus 4:21, Exodus 7:3,

Exodus 14:4, Exodus 14:17 but then these verses show us that God hardened Pharaoh's heart only after Pharaoh chose to harden his heart. That is to say God made sure that the hardening of heart of Pharaoh was firm after his own desire and actions. (Cf. Exodus 8:15, 19, 32, 34; 9:34)

"Wherefore then do ye harden your hearts, as the Egyptians and Pharaoh hardened their hearts? when he had wrought wonderfully among them, did they not let the people go, and they departed?" (1 Samuel 6:6)

God provided the circumstances and the occasion for Pharaoh to make a decision and Pharaoh made decision to harden his heart and God approved his decision. Pharaoh was guilty of his decision. Similarly, Pilate was guilty of his choice of handing over Jesus Christ to be crucified.

The LORD commanded Moses to say to the children of Israel to choose either blessing by following the LORD or to choose the curse by not following the LORD. As we see later Israel stumbled many times and was chastised severely.

PREDESTINATION | LESLIE JOHN

"I call heaven and earth to record this day against you, that I have set before you life and death, blessing and cursing: therefore choose life, that both thou and thy seed may live" (Deuteronomy30:19)

Prophet Hosea spoke the word of the LORD and said about the children of Israel that they were like prostitute cheating upon her husband. Paul picks up what Hosea spoke about them from Hosea Chapters 1-3 and quotes them in Romans 9:25 that the children of Israel were called as "Lo-ruhama" and "Lo-Ammi" which mean that the LORD will have no mercy upon the house of Israel and will utterly take them away (Hosea 1:6) and that they are not His people and He will not be their God (Hosea 1:9).

God does not leave them in such condition; but will have mercy upon them when they repent of their sin and turn to the LORD as we read in Hosea 1:10 and Hosea 2:1

"Yet the number of the children of Israel shall be as the sand of the sea, which cannot be measured nor numbered; and it shall come to pass, that in the place where it was said unto them, Ye are not my people, there it shall be said unto them, Ye are the sons of the living God". (Hosea 1:10)

"Say ye unto your brethren, Ammi; and to your sisters, Ruhamah" (Hosea 2:1).

A passage from Jeremiah 18:6-12 also shows us that man has choice to choose what he wants to choose and face the consequences and that God does not force upon him God's choices. God reveals to man His glory and the way to obtain salvation but the onus of accepting God's revelation and choosing of glory and salvation is on the man.

If only God forced upon man the salvation without giving any opportunity for man to decide for himself the salvation, the blessings, the conforming to the image of His Son, the very purpose of giving his disciples commission to preach the Gospel of Jesus Christ had no meaning. Surely God is sovereign, and man has no free will, because man cannot do anything against God by his own will, and yet wicked is left to exercise his choice to choose either salvation or destruction.

The wicked will be in hell by their own choice and it is not according to the purposes of God nor were they created or set apart to be so before the foundation of the world was laid by God.

God in his foreknowledge marked out those who would believe in Him to be conformed to the image of His Son and they are the ones who respond to the call of the Gospel of Jesus Christ.

The believers in Christ are chosen to be conformed to the image of Christ and that is yet to be fulfilled. The believers are given the status of adopted sons and as Apostle Paul writes in Galatians Chapter 4.

The heir is a child and does have more status than that of a servant though he is lord of all because he is still under tutors and governors until the time appointed by the father.

Similarly when the fullness of time was come God sent His only begotten Son, who was born of the virgin, made under law and we, who were under the bondage of sin, are redeemed from the Mosaic Law that we might receive the adoption of sons.

Now, because we the believers in Christ are the sons, God gave us the privilege to call the Father as "Abba, Father". Therefore, we have no more a status of a servant, but of a son, and because we have that status as son, we heirs of God through Christ (cf. Galatians 4:1-7).

Our bodies are made of dust and these bodies must return to dust. Until then we sweat and eat food that we have through our toil, and return to dust in the fullness of the time that God has appointed (cf. Genesis 3:19).

After we return to dust our spirit goes to be with the Lord. As the Scriptures say we must all appear before the judgment seat of Christ that we may receive the rewards, whether they are good or bad, that we have done in our bodies (cf. 2 Corinthians 5:6-11).

As we are in this world with the physical bodies that God has given us our bodies are subject to the consequences of our sin until these bodies are redeemed when the Lord comes again. The Lord himself descends from heaven with the voice of the archangel, and with the trump of God.

The dead will rise first and those who are alive then will be caught up together with them in the clouds to the meet the Lord in the air and be with the Lord for ever and ever. (cf. 1 Thessalonians 4:16-17).

Man is sinner by birth through Adam but will be made alive as the Scripture says: "For as in Adam all die, even so in Christ shall all be made alive". (1 Corinthians 15:22). It is a mystery revealed to us that we will not all die but shall be changed in a moment in the twinkling of an eye at the last trump when the trumpet sounds, and the dead are raised incorruptible. God gives us bodies according to His pleasure. 1 Corinthians 15:38, 51-52)

In Romans Chapter 8 to 11 Paul brings out sublime thoughts on how God gave the opportunity for Gentiles to come to His presence by blinding the understanding of Jews until the fullness of time of Gentiles be come in. The Jews in this dispensation of "Church", the body of Christ, whose head is the Lord Jesus Christ, should come to him just as Gentiles. There is no difference between Jews and Gentiles in this dispensation.

Those Jews who are defying God's commandments of accepting Jesus Christ as Messiah are missing heavenly blessings promised for believers in Christ in Ephesians Chapter 1. God chose a nation for himself and gave them His name and called them as "My People"

Old Testament prophets prophesied about the coming of the Messiah, and when Lord Jesus Christ, the Messiah came as prophesied they rejected Him.

They expected their Messiah would come like a king but Jesus came into this world in the form of a servant in the likeness of man to redeem them and also all of us from the bondage of sin by offering Himself as the sacrifice on the cross of Calvary.

There is no necessity to offer animals as sacrifice any more as those sacrifices only covered sins, but could not remit the sins fully. The blood of Jesus Christ shed for everyone is always available to cleanse from sins of anyone who accepts Him as the Messiah.

Confession of sins and accepting Lord Jesus Christ as one's Savior makes one the child of God and to have everlasting life.

The saved child of God will be with the Lord for ever having been conformed to the image of Christ that which is promised in the doctrine of Predestination presented in Romans Chapter 8:28-29 and in Ephesians Chapter 1.

However, those Jews, who have rejected Him as Savior and those in future, who would be left behind, after the Church (the body of Christ, also known as the "Bride of Christ" will be judged at the "Sheep and Goat Judgment" detailed in Matthew Chapter 25.

God deals with them in His own way and we are not authorized to judge their destiny. All that we are commanded to do is to "Pray for the peace of Jerusalem"

"Pray for the peace of Jerusalem: they shall prosper that love thee". (Psalms 122:6)

Lord Jesus Christ explained how the kingdom of heaven will be as we read in Matthew 20:1-16. It is like a man, a house holder, who went out early in the morning to hire laborers to work in his vineyard. He went in search of them early in the morning and hired laborers with an agreement that he would pay a penny a day.

The laborers agreed and went into work in his vineyard. The man went about the third hour and saw some other standing idle in the market place and said to them to go and work in his vineyard promising them their wages as are right in his sight. They went into work in his vineyard. Likewise, he hired some more at sixth hour, ninth hour and eleventh hour. Those who came into his vineyard were idling without work, but the man gave work to them in his compassion.

At the end of the day the man said to his steward to call all the laborers starting from those who were hired early in the morning to those who were hired at the eleventh hour. Remember the man entered into agreement to those who were hired early in the morning that he would pay them a penny a day and they agreed.

When it was time to distribute the wages the man paid to the laborers who came in to work at eleventh hour at the rate of a penny a day.

Then, those who came in to work early in the morning thought they would receive more than a penny a day as any man's logic in this would say. The lord of the vineyard gave every one equal wages according to His riches in his mercy without breaching upon the agreement made with those who came in to work early in the morning.

Those who came first into work in the vineyard murmured against the man who treated every one alike. But the man said to them that he did no wrong to them because lawfully he gave out of his abundance as he chose without breaking the agreement made with them. Similar would be the Kingdom of God, where the first would be made last and the last first as God decides. We are no judges to judge the actions of God and His mercy (cf. Matthew 20:1-16).

There are instances where we see God punished those who ill-treated Jews even though God called the children of Israel as "stiff necked". It is God who called them "stiff necked" but no man can take the advantage of God's calling them as "stiff necked" and call them so.

"For he saith to Moses, I will have mercy on whom I will have mercy, and I will have compassion on whom I will have compassion". (Romans 9:15)

Salvation belongs to the Lord Jesus Christ and He said "...I am the way, the truth, and the life: no man cometh unto the Father, but by me". (John 14:6)

Obviously, there is no way other than Lord Jesus Christ to have everlasting life and no man can go the Father except through Him.

No one can earn salvation through his good works or good behavior but the only way to everlasting life is to believe in the sacrificial death of Lord Jesus Christ for our sins and confess our sins to him. If you confess with your mouth the Lord Jesus Christ and believe in your heart that God raised him from the dead you will be saved.

"That if thou shalt confess with thy mouth the Lord Jesus, and shalt believe in thine heart that God hath raised him from the dead, thou shalt be saved" (Romans 10:9)

It is the only way to conformed to the image of Lord Jesus Christ in eternity. No one would want the image of fallen Adam, who, before the fall had all the glory in creation and was given dominion over the fish of the sea, over the fowl of the air, and over every living thing that moves on the earth although he was made of dust.

In his fall Adam lost many blessings and the earth was cursed for him. He was asked to toil hard and in his sweat he would earn food for him.

"And God blessed them, and God said unto them, Be fruitful, and multiply, and replenish the earth, and subdue it: and have dominion over the fish of the sea, and over the fowl of the air, and over every living thing that moveth upon the earth". (Genesis 1:28)

Whenever man is in comfortable and blessed state he tends to turn against the will of God. The children of Israel were given "manna" from heaven and protection from God when they were journeying in the wilderness but they murmured all the time. God commanded them not to worship any other idol but they made calf of gold and worshipped it.

Even after reaching Canaan, and many years later they worshipped Baal, and Ashtaroth in high places and angered Jehovah.

The children of Israel rebelled against the Jehovah not once or twice but several times until they were plucked out from the land of Israel and scattered throughout the world. God is waiting for them eagerly to return to Him but they chose to reject Jesus Christ as the Messiah.

Prophets spoke about Lord Jesus Christ, but when He was on this earth, they cried out before the Pilate that His blood may be upon them yet crucify Him. Rightly so, as they desired, Titus went and destroyed the whole land of Israel not leaving one stone upon the other of their blessed Temple Jerusalem, in AD 70.

The children of Israel were killed and harassed beyond anyone could imagine. They still choose to be under the Old Testament laws and yet not fully obeying all the Ten Commandments.

It was known fact that no one could keep all the Ten Commandments, neither was it possible to sacrifice animals for the covering of their sins year after year, yet they choose to follow what is in the Old Testament and fail on many counts.

Jesus came to fulfill the law and removed the yoke of circumcision, yoke of Mosaic Law, and ended the necessity of animal sacrifices, yet they choose to live under the yoke and fail to fulfill all that was required of them by God. Lord Jesus became propitiation for not only them but for all and died as substitution for all mankind.

Whoever confesses his sins to Lord Jesus Christ He will not only forgive their sins, but justify the one who confesses his sing to him, as pure, righteous, and holy. It is so unfortunate that the children of Israel, whom God loved so much and called them as "My People" still, stand in rebellion against God and do not accept Jesus Christ as their Messiah.

If only they accepted Jesus as their savior and as the Son of God and believed Him as Savior, God was willing to conform them to the image of Lord Jesus Christ, but they choose to live under the yoke of Old Testament laws and have earthly blessings rather than heavenly blessings promised to the "body of Christ". Hebrews 10:26 says that if we sin willfully after receiving the knowledge of the truth there is more sacrifices left for neither Jew nor Gentile for the remission of sins. It is only the belief in the sacrificial death of Lord Jesus Christ that can save a man from perishing.

"For if we sin wilfully after that we have received the knowledge of the truth, there remaineth no more sacrifice for sins" (Hebrews 10:26)

Lord Jesus Christ became propitiation and substitution and promised to justify anyone who comes to Him and accept Him as Lord and Savior, but then Jews still remain in rebellion to the invitation He gave them. Lord Jesus Christ died upon the cross of Calvary bearing sins of every one and yet the Jews desire to be under Old Covenant.

It is proved beyond doubt that it is impossible to keep all the Ten Commandments given by the God through Moses, yet, they prefer to remain under them. When the Church, the body of Christ, the bride of Christ is caught up on Jesus coming again, they would be left behind still in rebellion to the invitation of accepting Him as the Messiah.

After the resurrection and ascension of Lord Jesus Christ the Gospel message was being proclaimed by His disciples when there came down from Judea and taught the brethren that they should be circumcised as Mosaic Law prescribed otherwise, they said, there would not be salvation. This was nothing but laying heavy yoke on those who are freed by Lord Jesus Christ.

Salvation is purely by the grace of God through faith in Him and accepting Lord Jesus Christ as Savior and by confessing sins to Him that He may forgive them. But the Pharisees and Scribes lay heavy burden on the people that Mosaic Law should still be observed to receive salvation.

PREDESTINATION | LESLIE JOHN

When Paul and Barnabas came to know about such insistence, there arose no small dissensions and disputation with them. In the council at Jerusalem it was resolved even with Peter endorsing the teaching of Paul is according the desire of Lord Jesus Christ (Acts 15:1-5)

The realization that Lord Jesus Christ is the Messiah and the stringent Mosaic Law is outdated comes in them only when they are subject to the "Great Tribulation" under Antichrist, and every knee will bow then to Lord Jesus Christ and accept Him as the Messiah.

CHAPTER 3 ADOPTION

While dealing with this subject of predestination it becomes necessary to expound few verses.

"For whom he did foreknow, he also did predestinate to be conformed to the image of his Son, that he might be the firstborn among many brethren. Moreover whom he did predestinate, them he also called: and whom he called, them he also justified: and whom he justified, them he also glorified". (Romans 8:29-30)

God said as many as are led by the Spirit of God, they are the sons of God and the sons of God have not received the spirit of bondage again to fear but received the spirit of adoption. This privilege entails us to call God as "Abba, Father" and the Spirit bears witness that we are the children of God. (Romans 8:14-16).

Apostle Paul explains that the heir as long as he is a child does not differ from a servant because even though he is the lord of all, he is under tutor and governors until the time appointed of the father.

The children are still considered as in bondage under the elements of the world. But when the fullness of time was come God sent His one only begotten Son, born of the virgin Mary, conceived of the Holy Ghost, made under law, to redeem that was under the law that we might receive the adoption of sons.

Therefore, we are no more servants but sons and daughters, and if it is so, then we are heirs of God through Christ. Lord Jesus Christ redeemed us from the bondage of Mosaic Law and gave us the liberty to be under the provisions of Gospel to gain the privilege of being the adopted sons and receive the full benefits promised to the children of Israel.

Even though the promises, covenants and law belonged to the children of Israel, yet, now those who accept Lord Jesus Christ as savior are set free from the stringent Laws of Moses. Our salvation is by grace through faith. (Galatians 4:1-7).

It was according to God's good pleasure of His will that Gentiles are also made equal partners of the inheritance of heavenly blessings.

Now, therefore, in this dispensation there is no difference between Jew and Gentile. A Jew has to come to the Lord Jesus Christ just as any Gentile would come and accept Him as the Savior.

Jesus is the only way, the Truth, and the Life and no one can come to the Father except through Him. If Jews need heavenly blessings and are desirous of being conformed, in future, to the image of Lord Jesus Christ, who relinquished His glory

when He came into this world as a servant in the form of man, was crucified, died, buried and rose from the dead with uncorrupted body, in his glorified body, ascended into heaven, and seated on the right hand of the Majesty, then they necessarily have to accept Lord Jesus Christ as their Messiah.

If they continue to be in rebellion of the Gospel of Jesus Christ, then, according to the word of God, they lose that privilege of being conformed to the image of His Son in eternity.

"Having predestinated us unto the adoption of children by Jesus Christ to himself, according to the good pleasure of his will" (Ephesians 1:5)

"In whom also we have obtained an inheritance, being predestinated according to the purpose of him who worketh all things after the counsel of his own will" (Ephesians 1:11)

God predestines us unto the adoption as children by Lord Jesus Christ to Himself according to the good pleasure of His will. In Him we have obtained an inheritance according to the purpose of Him.

The very first assertion the scripture makes here is that God foreknew those who would be conformed to the image of his Son, Lord Jesus Christ.

Therefore, God predestined those who, in his foreknowledge, would respond to His call and accept Lord Jesus Christ as their savior. Those, who respond and confess their sins to Lord Jesus Christ, will be forgiven of their sins and justified.

They are assured of being confirmed, in future, to the image of his son and, therefore, He called them and will glorify them in eternity.

Surely God foreknew those who would be conformed to the image of his Son. Therefore, he called them and justified and glorified them. None of these assertions add emphasis to imaginations that God predestined some to hell or God forcibly converts any human to his side.

The Bible contains message of Gospel of Jesus Christ and the message is that Lord Jesus Christ is the Savior, that He is the Son of God, that He and the Father are one, and that there is no salvation outside of Him. Jesus is the way, the truth and the light.

"And not only they, but ourselves also, which have the firstfruits of the Spirit, even we ourselves groan within ourselves, waiting for the adoption, to wit, the redemption of our body" (Romans 8:23)

"Who are Israelites; to whom pertaineth the adoption, and the glory, and the covenants, and the giving of the law, and the service of God, and the promises" (Romans 9:4)

"To redeem them that were under the law, that we might receive the adoption of sons" (Galatians 4:5)

It was God's good pleasure that according to His will he predestined us unto adoption of children by Jesus Christ. Man has no free will to do anything against the will of God to be predestined either to become the child of God or to go against God.

It is God who controls men's will. Man can by himself do nothing other than choosing for himself eternal damnation by rejecting Jesus as Savior. There is difference between choice a man makes and the will that he has. Men's will is not free to make any decision against God's will but men can make their choices. The will of Men cannot overpower God's will. The will of God is all powerful and God makes the world to move according to His will, and yet he provides a choice and chance for man to repent of his sin and choose the living God. Jehovah is living God and not an idol. Idols do not move, do not speak, and do not do anything on their own.

Jehovah is the living God who loved us and gave His one and only begotten Son to be crucified for our sake in order that we might be saved from perishing. Whosoever believes in Jesus as Savior will not perish but will have everlasting life.

There is inheritance promised to those who believe in Lord Jesus Christ as Savior and we are predestinated to have that inheritance in future and to be conformed to the image of His Son.

This is according to the purpose of Him who works all things according to the counsel of His own will. Jehovah does not need our counsel and His counsel and His purposes are final.

The image of God is lost in the Garden of Eden when man committed transgression against the will of God and sinned against God's law. God is the creator and man is under His will and His purposes, yet man has the choice to choose the better or worse.

The first man exercised his choice in a bad way and lost the image of God. In His mercy God desires to restore that lost image to all those who have sinned. Bible says there is no one righteous; not even one and every one has come short of the glory of God. If we say that we have not sinned, then we make God a liar. The only way to get out of that bad situation and to be conformed to the image of the Son, Lord Jesus Christ, is to repent of sins and turn to God and accept that Lord Jesus Christ is the only Savior.

CHAPTER 4 SALVATION

THE CURSE FROM GOD FOLLOWED

The LORD God cursed the earth for man; the woman with pain in her child labor, and God cursed serpent that the serpent would crawl all the days of his life.

This resulted in Adam toiling for food; woman who was in Adam and who became his wife to be a help-mate was cursed with pain in her child-bearing. The serpent that was not crawling before became a most loathed reptile on the earth to crawl on the earth his entire life. God put enmity between the seed of the woman and of the serpent.

Adam called the woman as "Eve" because she was the mother of all living. This is how the sin entered the world. In order to reconcile man to God, Jesus relinquished his glory in heaven and came down into this world in the form of man and lived among us.

"And I will put enmity between thee and the woman, and between thy seed and her seed; it shall bruise thy head, and thou shalt bruise his heel". (Genesis 3:15)

GOD SENT HIS ONLY BEGOTTEN SON

"For God so loved the world, that he gave his only begotten Son, that whosoever believeth in him should not perish, but have everlasting life" (John 3:16)

Jesus said: "Therefore doth my Father love me, because I lay down my life, that I might take it again". (John 10:17)

SALVATION IS FREE OF COST

According to Bible good works alone will not get us into heaven but faith in Lord Jesus Christ alone saves us. Confession by mouth and the belief that God raised Him from the dead will get us salvation free of cost. Salvation is free. No amount of good works can get a person a place in heaven. The works will follow faith in Jesus Christ and salvation.

Let the Word of God speak to our hearts Heavenly Father's love is shown in John Chapter 3:16. He sent His only begotten Son, Jesus Christ for our sake that whosoever believes in him should not perish but have everlasting life.

There is a clause which is conditional here. The condition is that a person has to believe that The Father has sent His only begotten Son, Jesus Christ into this world for the remission of our sins. The purpose of sending Jesus into this world was that whoever believes in Him through Jesus Christ he will have everlasting life.

The initial mission of Jesus was to seek the lost sheep of Israel. Jesus also said to his twelve disciples not to go into the way of the Gentiles and into any city of Samaritans.

This was the time when Jesus preached the Kingdom of heaven. (Matthew 10:5-6).

Later in Mathew Chapter 15 we see that a Gentile woman from Canaan approached Jesus and prayed to him addressing him as "O Lord, thou Son of David" and crying out to have mercy on her because her daughter was grievously vexed with a devil. Jesus did not answer her testing her faith but when his disciples interceded to send her away because she was crying, Jesus answered and said he was not sent but unto the lost sheep of the house of the Israel.

This should not be misunderstood that Jesus came into this world only for the sake of Jews. It is indeed true that his first priority was to seek the lost sheep of Israel. Until his crucifixion Jesus was under the Law of Moses. It was divine plan that Jesus should keep the Law of Moses meticulously; yet Jesus being the Son of God, had compassion on the Gentile woman that her faith was great and granted to her answer to her prayer and her daughter was made whole from that very hour. (Matthew 15:22-28).

Jesus nailed the handwritten laws and ordinances of Moses at the cross because they were contrary to the Gentiles. Those ordinances were blotted out as Apostle Paul wrote in Colossians 2:14. The message of Salvation is sent out to everyone on the earth after resurrection of Jesus Christ as per the commission given by Jesus in Matthew Chapter 28:19-20 and Acts 1:8

David wrote in Psalm 28:1 "Unto thee will I cry, O LORD my rock; be not silent to me: lest, if thou be silent to me, I become like them that go down into the pit" God will answer our prayers when we pray with faith. In the Gospel according to John Chapter 10 God's love is shown toward all those who believe in him. There is a security of salvation assured. Jesus is the Good Shepherd.

Jesus said: "Therefore doth my Father love me, because I lay down my life, that I might take it again". (John 10:17). The believer in Christ is not redeemed with corruptible things such as silver and gold or from vain conversations of forefathers but by the precious blood of Lord Jesus Christ. (1 Peter 1:18)

God had sent Jesus Christ to be a propitiation for us and whoever believes in him shall be redeemed of his sin and justified before him. (Romans 3:25, 1 John 2:2)

"Herein is love, not that we loved God, but that he loved us, and sent his Son to be the propitiation for our sins".1 John 4:10

"In whom we have redemption through his blood, the forgiveness of sins, according to the riches of his grace" Ephesians 1:7

"And that he might reconcile both unto God in one body by the cross, having slain the enmity thereby" Ephesians 2:16

"In whom we have redemption through his blood, even the forgiveness of sins" Colossians 1:14

"And, having made peace through the blood of his cross, by him to reconcile all things unto himself; by him, I say, whether they be things in earth, or things in heaven". Colossians 1:20

God loved us first and not that we did first. That is the reason why, though we trespassed His commandments, He sent His one and only Son, Jesus Christ to die on our stead.

JESUS CONQURED SATAN

"So Christ was once offered to bear the sins of many; and unto them that look for him shall he appear the second time without sin unto salvation". Hebrews 9:28

"That if thou shalt confess with thy mouth the Lord Jesus, and shalt believe in thine heart that God hath raised him from the dead, thou shalt be saved". Romans 10:9

"Whom God hath raised up, having loosed the pains of death: because it was not possible that he should be holden of it". (Acts 2:24)

"But ye shall receive power, after that the Holy Ghost is come upon you: and ye shall be witnesses unto me both in Jerusalem, and in all Judaea, and in Samaria, and unto the uttermost part of the earth. And when he had spoken these things, while they beheld, he was taken up; and a cloud received him out of their sight. And while they looked stedfastly toward heaven as he went up, behold, two men stood by them in white apparel; Which also said, Ye men of Galilee, why stand ye gazing up into heaven? this same Jesus, which is taken up from you into heaven, shall so come in like manner as ye have seen him go into heaven." (Acts 1:8-11)

Jesus died for our sake; he was buried, and was raised from the dead. Jesus, who is the seed of the woman, crushed the head of the serpent at the cross. Jesus rose from the dead on the third day and he appeared before many. Death could not hold him in the grave and He conquered death. Later after forty days he ascended into heaven. Jesus will come again in the same manner he ascended into heaven.

It is a wrong notion that God prepared vessels of wrath before the foundation of the world in order to glorify the vessels of mercy. If we take into consideration the statistics of ever growing population in the world that includes God's chosen people, the Israel, and the deaths that have occurred from first century onwards it is unbelievable that many still say God predestinated so many billions of people for destruction.

God's love towards man is exceedingly great and His offering of His only begotten Son as sacrifice for the remission of our sins is grossly misinterpreted by some to add the advantage only to those limited ones, who, they believe, would respond to the call of God irresistibly.

Bible asserts that God is love and it is He who loved us first, not that we loved Him first. God predestinated us in his foreknowledge and called us to believe in Him, but the onus of believing on Lord Jesus Christ as one's personal savior is on man.

"Jesus saith unto him, I am the way, the truth, and the life: no man cometh unto the Father, but by me". (John 14:6)

"For God so loved the world, that he gave his only begotten Son, that whosoever believeth in him should not perish, but have everlasting life" John 3:16

While it is true that no one comes to the Father except through Lord Jesus Christ it is also true that only those who believe in Lord Jesus Christ shall not perish, but have everlasting life. The responsibility of believing in Lord Jesus Christ rests on man. God does not force anyone to believe in Him nor does man respond irresistibly to God's call. At the same time man's will is not greater than God's will and man cannot by himself do anything against the will of God.

Apostle Paul wrote those words in Romans 8:29-30 and Ephesians 1:5, 11 for the edification of believers in Christ; not in any way to cause divisions among Christians. The Scriptures give us great hope of being confirmed to the Son of God, Lord Jesus Christ, but this is yet future.

The prophecies are written in past tense and many of them are fulfilled and many of them are yet to be fulfilled. The hope given to the believers in Christ that they will be confirmed to the image of His Son is yet to be fulfilled.

It is interesting to note that Satan takes out the same phrases that God intended as hope for the believers and uses them to cause divisions among them. Satan side tracks the issue at hand and puts believers into debate as to whether God predestinated some to salvation and some to destruction. Consequently one section of the believers keeps arguing that God predestined some to salvation and the rest to destruction.

There is another section of believers, who argue that God predestinated some to salvation and we should not say God predestined others for destruction. The debate continues and man struggles to evolve a solution ultimately bringing dishonor to God and honor to Satan. That is what Satan intends to do.

MESSAGE OF SALVATION

By offering Himself upon the cross of Calvary, Jesus opened the way for everyone to be saved. Jesus died for our sake as atonement for our sins. He was the perfect sacrifice. Jesus saved "whosoever believeth in him should not perish, but have everlasting life".

Jesus, who is righteous, declares us righteous upon our confession of our sins. Through the blood of Jesus Christ we have the redemption and the forgiveness of our sins. It pleased the Father to bruise him for sake and He did that according to his riches in Grace. Grace alone saves us. We are redeemed from our sins and have obtained forgiveness of our sins through Jesus Christ.

Jesus died upon the cross of Calvary so that we may be reconciled unto Him. There is no difference whether we are Jews or Gentiles we are all one in Christ. Jesus died for all of us, and he rose from the dead and ascended in to heaven. We, who were His enemies, are made His children.

The opposition that was caused between God and Man by man's sin is reconciled once and for all by Jesus Christ dying on the cross for our sake.

We are reconciled unto God through His blood that was shed upon the cross of Calvary. All that we have to do is to believe that Jesus is the Lord.

CHAPTER 5

IS LAW NAILED ON THE CROSS?

"Now therefore why tempt ye God, to put a yoke upon the neck of the disciples, which neither our fathers nor we were able to bear?" (Acts 15:10)

Who would want an inferior position that is earned through hard struggle when an exalted position is available easily? It is similar to this when Jews prefer to follow the Old Testament provisions while God has provided an easy method of procuring heavenly blessings through Lord Jesus Christ.

The Father gives to all those who are predestined to be confirmed to be in the image of His Son, glorified bodies, who rule from New Jerusalem that comes down from heaven. All those who are left-behind will be in earthly bodies on this earth to be ruled over.

It is as simple as accepting Lord Jesus Christ as personal Savior by confessing sins to Him. Those who will be caught up into mid-air to meet Lord Jesus Christ when He comes for His bride will be in the glorified bodies conformed to the image of Christ. Lord Jesus Christ with His bride, the Church, the body of Christ, steps on to the mount olives and then after 'Sheep and Goat' judgment the Lord will rule over those who are on this earth.

The reign will be for thousand years. What a privilege is being lost by those who are called as "My People" by God that they are choosing to be on the earth with earthly bodies to be ruled over by Lord Jesus Christ and those that are confirmed to the image of Him.

"For the Lord himself shall descend from heaven with a shout, with the voice of the archangel, and with the trump of God: and the dead in Christ shall rise first: Then we which are alive and remain shall be caught up together with them in the clouds, to meet the Lord in the air: and so shall we ever be with the Lord". (1 Thessalonians 4:16-17)

"Behold, I shew you a mystery; We shall not all sleep, but we shall all be changed, In a moment, in the twinkling of an eye, at the last trump: for the trumpet shall sound, and the dead shall be raised incorruptible, and we shall be changed. For this corruptible must put on incorruption, and this mortal must put on immortality. So when this corruptible shall have put on incorruption, and this mortal shall have put on immortality, then shall be brought to pass the saying that is written, Death is swallowed up in victory" (1 Corinthians 15:51-54)

"For whom he did foreknow, he also did predestinate to be conformed to the image of his Son, that he might be the firstborn among many brethren". (Romans 8:29)

" Blotting out the handwriting of ordinances that was against us, which was contrary to us, and took it out of the way, nailing it to his cross" Colossians 2:14 (KJV)

There is a misconception that Jesus nailed the Law on the cross and abolished it. At the very start of His ministry on this earth, while preaching the Sermon on the Mount, as recorded in Matthew Chapters 5-7, Jesus made it very clear that He did not come to abolish the Law, but to fulfill it.

"Think not that I am come to destroy the law, or the prophets: I am not come to destroy, but to fulfil. For verily I say unto you, Till heaven and earth pass, one jot or one tittle shall in no wise pass from the law, till all be fulfilled" (Matthew 5:17-18)

If it so, what is that then Apostle Paul writes in Colossians 2:14?

An easier understanding of the verse is:

"having canceled the charge of our legal indebtedness, which stood against us and condemned us; he has taken it away, nailing it to the cross" Colossians 2:14 (NIV)

Or,

"by canceling the record of debt that stood against us with its legal demands. This he set aside, nailing it to the cross" Colossians 2:14 (ESV)

It is wrong notion that Jesus nailed the Law on the cross; no, He did not. Law surely pointed guilt of a person. By observing Mosaic Law none of us can be saved. Salvation is by grace through faith.

What is achieved on the cross was not abolition of the Law or nailing of the Law on the cross, but the abolition of debts of sinners that stood against them. The legal demands of the Law were nailed to the cross and wiped out. In other words, Jesus set aside the record of these debts on the cross; it is this record that was abolished. If Jesus nailed the Law, it is equivalent of saying that Jesus failed in His mission.

In fact Jesus set us on higher plane of the Law to follow the demands of law, by saying that lusting after woman is equivalent to committing adultery. A man calling his brother "Raca", shall be in danger of the council; a man calling another "Thou fool, shall be in danger of hell fire".

At this rate none of us can be saved. It is all by the grace of God that saves us.

"But I say unto you, That whosoever is angry with his brother without a cause shall be in danger of the judgment: and whosoever shall say to his brother, Raca, shall be in danger of the council: but whosoever shall say, Thou fool, shall be in danger of hell fire". (Matthew 5:22)

Jews contented with Gentiles on one main reason that the latter did not keep the Law. There was physical barrier, the actual "wall of separation" between them, in the temple, separating Jew from Gentile.

The Gentiles were aliens to the commonwealth of Israel. By the blood of Jesus Christ offered on the cross He reconciled them together to make them "One New Man" in Christ.

The finished work of Lord Jesus Christ on the cross is the reason for reconciling Jews with Gentiles. He brought them together. He did not abolish the Law, but fulfilled the law for this purpose, and this is the common ground for the salvation of Jews and Gentiles.

No one could receive salvation by keeping the Law; but every sinner could be saved by believing in Jesus Christ, who canceled the list of our sins on the cross. (cf. Ephesians 2:13,16)

"Christ hath redeemed us from the curse of the law, being made a curse for us: for it is written, Cursed is every one that hangeth on a tree" (Galatians 3:13)

"For he is our peace, who hath made both one, and hath broken down the middle wall of partition between us; Having abolished in his flesh the enmity, even the law of commandments contained in ordinances; for to make in himself of twain one new man, so making peace" (Ephesians 2:14-15)

CHAPTER 6 ATONEMENT

"For Christ is not entered into the holy places made with hands, which are the figures of the true; but into heaven itself, now to appear in the presence of God for us: Nor yet that he should offer himself often, as the high priest entereth into the holy place every year with blood of others" (Hebrews 9:24-25)

Usually man views his present status lightly unless he compares it with his previous status from where he was elevated.

He would give least importance to his present status if had forgotten the troubles and trials that he had undergone in rising up from his old status to the present status. He might think that he deserved all the blessings and they are all by his own virtue and his efforts.

Most of the Christians feel comfortable with the freedom that they have in approaching the Father through Lord Jesus Christ without realizing that God was so unapproachable in the Old Testament period. The study of priests, high priest and the offerings and sacrifices that they had offer year after year will help Christians to appreciate the freedom they enjoy in Christ.

While the priests offered sacrifices several times a year on several occasions the high priest was authorized to enter the "Holy of Holies" only once a year to offer sin offering in a very meticulous method that God prescribed. He risked his own life while making an entry into the Holy of Holies; first with incense, second with the blood of the Lord's goat. He then confessed the sins of the people by placing his hands on live goat If the high priest made any mistake in doing these ceremonies the result would be his instant death.

God gave so specific instructions to Aaron, the high priest, through Moses, His servant that any violation of it even to the minutest detail would invite his own death. Every bit of instruction was to be followed meticulously without any negligence. The LORD spoke to Moses, after the death of Nadab and Abihu, who were the sons of Aaron, the brother of Moses that Aaron should not enter not more than once a year into Holy of Holies where the mercy seat, which is upon the ark of the testament is located. If he committed any violation in this commandment, then he would die. There was none to be present except the high priest within the whole tabernacle on the 'Day of Atonement' when the national repentance is made.

Aaron was commanded to remove his priestly garments and wash his flesh in water and wear linen coat, the linen breeches upon his flesh and with a linen girdle, and with a linen miter before he makes the sin offering. He was to enter into the sanctuary, which is the holy place, with a young bullock for a sin offering and a ram for a burnt offering. He shall take of people of Israel to kids of goats for a sin offering a ram for burnt offering.

According to Scriptures every man is a sinner by birth and come short of the glory of God.

"For all have sinned, and come short of the glory of God" (Romans 3:23)

"Wherefore, as by one man sin entered into the world, and death by sin; and so death passed upon all men, for that all have sinned" (Romans 5:12)

As God is holy no man could approach Him unless reconciliation was made in the way that was prescribed by God. Man is God's creation and, therefore, he is subject to the authority of God. God's law always prevailed and will prevail even unto the ends of man no matter what man thinks of it. Man has, therefore, no authority to question God as to how He his way are and how conducts himself with His creation.

It is His pleasure and, therefore, man's obedience to God's law is mandatory. Man is created to worship God and every knee shall bow to Him, either willingly or forcibly. There is nothing like a third option while choosing God or Satan. Either man has to choose God or Satan. If man chooses to worship God he has everlasting life and blessings, and if man chooses to worship Satan he has everlasting torment in the 'lake of fire'.

FELLOWSHIP

Loving as He is, God always cherished fellowship with man and desired to commune with him. With Adam and Eve falling into sin they lost fellowship with God and consequently we all have inherited that sin from him. God provided way to go near him and have fellowship with Him provided our sins are put away from us and righteousness is imputed to us. The imputation is righteousness to man is possible only at the discretion of God when all the conditions that He prescribed are fulfilled.

These conditions were in different form in the Old Testament period than that of New Testament period. We would not have realized the benefits we have in Jesus Christ unless we knew the pattern of worship that was laid out for man in the Old Testament. Every bit of worship of the Old Testament was shadow that was fulfilled in the New Testament. It is therefore, essential that we should not discard reading and understanding Old Testament. There is no way for man to get rid of his sin unless the prescribed sacrifice is offered to God and its blood is shed.

John the Baptist said of Lord Jesus Christ He was the Lamb of God who takes away the sin of the world. The Law was given by Moses, but grace and truth came by Jesus Christ (John 1:17, John 1:29). There is only one way for salvation. Jesus is the way, the truth and the life. (John 14:6). Speaking to Nicodemus Jesus said "…Verily, verily, I say unto thee, Except a man be born again, he cannot see the kingdom of God" (John 3:3).

"For God so loved the world, that he gave his only begotten Son, that whosoever believeth in him should not perish, but have everlasting life". (John 3:16)

In Jesus Christ the law was fulfilled and He was the anti-type of the shadow that was observed in the Old Testament period. The sacrifices and offerings made in the Old Testament period covered their sins but were never fully blotted out until Jesus died for our sake.

When Jesus was crucified on the Cross the veil in the temple was rent from top to bottom signifying that the Old Testament type of sacrifices was done away and Jesus became the sacrifice once and for all. Jesus became our high priest of the order of Melchisedec and the only mediator between us and the Father.

Later after forty days Lord Jesus Christ ascended into heaven and seated at the right hand of the Majesty. He will come back again in the same manner he ascended into heaven after all His enemies are brought to His footstool. (Psalm 110:1). For the salvation of man it is now necessary only to believe in Jesus as the Lord, and in his crucifixion, burial, resurrection, and ascension. The salvation is by faith by grace alone and not by any works or any kind of sacrifices.

Year after year and once in every year the high priest had to repeat the prescribed method of offering sacrifices to God on the "Day of Atonement" The people of Israel did not have direct access to God but they had to be represented by priests and high priest.

While the priests could be their representatives for offering their sacrifices on other occasions, the only person authorized to offer 'sin offering' on the 'Day of Atonement' was the high priest. This day is also called "Yom Kippur". The burnt offering was made only after the sin offering was made.

The sacrifices on the 'Day of Atonement' were made by the high priest as the LORD Commanded Aaron through Moses. God was so unapproachable in the Old Testament period that even Aaron, the high priest could not have instructions straight from God. The LORD gave instructions to Aaron through Moses, his servant.

The LORD said to Moses to instruct Aaron that he should not go into the "Holy of Holies" of the Tabernacle at all times and if he failed he will surely die. The LORD said that He will appear in the cloud upon the mercy seat that is on the ark in the Most Holy Place also called "Holy of Holies".

Before His crucifixion, Jesus ate the Passover. "And he took the cup, and gave thanks, and said, Take this, and divide it among yourselves" (Luke 22:17)

"And he took bread, and gave thanks, and brake it, and gave unto them, saying, This is my body which is given for you: this do in remembrance of me. Likewise also the cup after supper, saying, This cup is the new testament in my blood, which is shed for you." (Luke 22:19-20)

We now have the boldness to enter into His presence and worship Him freely in Spirit and in Truth. Jesus died for our sake, was buried and rose from the dead on the third day and appeared unto many and gave instructions to his disciples.

"But now hath he obtained a more excellent ministry, by how much also he is the mediator of a better covenant, which was established upon better promises". (Hebrews 8:6)

THE SACRIFICES

One Bullock for the high priest to offer as sacrifice for his own sins while he was in garments of linen and thereafter a ram as burnt offering while he was in priestly garments.

Two kids of Goats: One for the Lord and another for confessing sins upon. The Lord's goat is chosen by casting lot.

Aaron the High priest brings two kids of goats and present them before the LORD at the door of the tabernacle and shall cast lots upon the two kids of goats to determine which one of the two is for the LORD to be offered as sin offering, and which other one would be the scapegoat, otherwise also known as "Azazel" to carry the sins confessed upon him by the high priest, into the wilderness once and for all never to return. (Interesting to note that the casting of the lots also confirms another fact it was not wrong to choose 12th disciple as Matthias in place of Judas Iscariot [Cf. Acts 1:26]).

Aaron also will bring a ram for burnt offering. The LORD's goat is sacrificed on the altar as the sin offering and the scapegoat carries the iniquities of the people into the wilderness. The offerings are:

The fire from off the altar before the LORD, and his hands full of sweet incense beaten small, and bring it within the veil.

The blood of young bullock to be taken into the Holy Holies

The blood of Lord's goat for sin offering to be taken into the Holy of Holies

The blood of the bullock and the blood of the Lord's Goat in a single bowl to make atonement for the altar by applying it on the horns of the altar round about and then sprinkling the blood upon the altar with his finger seven times and cleanse it and hollow it from the uncleanness of the children of Israel.

The live goat to carry the sins to uninhabited land

The blood of ram for burnt offering for himself and for the people.

GARMENTS FOR THE HIGH PRIEST

The high priest had to put off his regular priestly clothing such as ephod, miter, etc. and wear holy linen coat and a linen girdle on the Day of Atonement while offering sin offering. He was to have his body cleansed in water before putting on those holy garments. He changes again to his priestly garments and offers the burnt offering for himself and for the people.

PLACE WHERE THE SACFICES ARE TO BE OFFERED

The bullock, the Lord's goat, and the ram are offered as sacrifices on the bronze altar in the outer court of the Tabernacle.

1.   The fire from off the altar before the LORD, and his hands full of sweet incense beaten small, and bring it within the veil and offers on the mercy seat, which is on the Ark of the Covenant.

2.   The confession of sins upon the live goat by the high priest in the tabernacle before the Lord at the Bronze altar.

3.   The blood of the ram on the in the Holy of Holies.

4.   The blood of the bullock and the goat together at the Bronze altar on the horns.

5.   The burning of the skins, and the flesh and dung of the bullock and the Lord's goat outside the camp and someone who assists the high priest

THE METHOD

The method that was followed to offer the sacrifices was very cumbersome and tedious, and yet, obedience was necessary; otherwise the death of the person offering sacrifice was sure and instant. The seriousness of offering strange fire before the LORD that He did not command, on other occasions by Nadab and Abihu, sons of Aaron, brought death upon them instantaneously. God did not take any method lightly nor did He pardon any one's errors in the offerings made unto Him, least would He have tolerated if high priest committed any mistake on the very important day such as the 'Day of Atonement'.

THE SEQUENCE

1.   The high priest will be all alone in the Tabernacle while performing the ceremonies on the 'Day of Atonement'. He washes his flesh in water and puts on the linen garments.

2.   The high priest was to take the bullock of the sin offering and make an atonement for him and for his house and kill it as sin offering on the altar. He was to take a censer full of burning coals of fire from off the altar before the LORD, and his hands full of sweet incense beaten small, and bring it within the veil. He shall put the incense upon the fire before the LORD, so that the cloud of the incense may cover the mercy seat that is upon the ark of the testimony; and if he failed to follow the said method his death was sure.

3.   The high priest shall take the blood of the bullock, and sprinkle it with his finger upon the mercy seat eastward, and he shall also sprinkle the blood before the mercy seat with his finger seven times.

4.   The high priest goes back to the altar and kills the goat on which the lot fell as sin offering for the people. The high priest takes the blood of the goat within the veil and applies the blood and sprinkle just as he did with the blood of bullock for his own sake.

5.   Because the Tabernacle remained in the midst of the children of Israel with all their transgressions and uncleanness Aaron, the high priest makes atonement for the holy place.

6.   The high priest shall bring the live goat and lays both his hands upon the head of the live goat, signifying the transference of the sins of himself, and all the people of Israel on to the live goat, and confess over the live goat all the iniquities of the children of Israel, and all the transgressions in all their sins, and shall send him away by the hand of the fit man into the wilderness.

a.   The goat carries the iniquities of all the people of Israel unto a land not inhabited never to return again to the land where the children of Israel lived. The live goat on which the sins are confessed is led outside the camp by a fit man into the wilderness. He, who lets the goat into the wilderness bathes his flesh in water and afterwards come into the camp.

b.   Notice the shedding of the blood and its sprinkling pardoned the sins of the sins, yet the sins remained in the sanctuary until the high priest transferred the sins onto the live goat which carried the sins far into an uninhabited land.

c.   The letting of the scapegoat into the wilderness is after the high priest changes his garments of linen and puts on his priestly garments and offering of the fat of the sin offering to be burnt upon the altar.

7.   After the sin offering is made by the high priest he shall go into the tabernacle of the congregation and shall change his clothing. The high priest washes his clothes, and bathe his flesh in water and then he goes into the camp in his priestly garments offers burnt offering..

8.   The high priest offers burnt offering for himself first and then offer burnt offering for the people and make atonement for himself and for the people. He burns the fat of the sin offering on the altar and then lets the scapegoat go. He washes his clothes bathes his flesh in water and afterward goes into the camp

9.   The rest of the blood of the bullock and the Lord's goat which were killed for making atonement for sin offering will be carried outside the camp. The skins, their flesh, and their dung shall but burnt in the fire. He who burns the skins their flesh, dung washes his clothes and

bathes his flesh in water and then shall come into the camp (Lev 16:27, 28).

10.   This ritual is ordered by God as a statute to be observed on the tenth day of every seventh month in every year. God ordered that the children of Israel should mourn on this day. This is only one festival where the children of Israel are asked to mourn instead of rejoicing. It is the 'Day of Atonement", which is a national repentance day. They and the strangers in that land and the sojourners in that land were not supposed to work on this day

11.   The priest whom the high priest anoints on this day will serve as the High priest next in the stead of his father. He shall make atonement for the holy sanctuary, tabernacle, and the altar, and also priests, and for all the people of the congregation.

12.   This ritual was ordered to be a statute to be observed once every year and Aaron did as the LORD gave commandment through Moses.

CHAPTER 7 ELECTION BY GRACE

Think about an officer who has total control over his staff and unlimited liberty to choose any one for any position in his organization. The question then is why anyone would consider his choosing someone for a job who in his opinion is best fit for that job as injustice?

The officer was not doing any injustice to others while he chose the best fit person for the job he wants to execute. Obviously, there should be no contention about his choice because he was vested with ultimate authority and unlimited liberty over the affairs of his organization.

If that is true in this secular world how true it should be in the case of the one who created this universe and everything in it. The creator owns everything and He has the right to do anything. He is sovereign. There is no injustice on his part on anything He does.

"Hath not the potter power over the clay, of the same lump to make one vessel unto honour, and another unto dishonour?" (Romans 9:21)

Apostle Paul questions those who have questions about God's sovereignty citing an example of potter who has the authority over the clay. His question is whether or not the potter has the power over the clay to make from the same lump one vessel unto honor and another unto dishonor. Surely the potter has the authority and liberty to make different kinds of vessels for different purposes some which can be used for good purposes and some would be for carrying dirt.

Whatever the potter he does it is for some use and nothing for discarding. Then why would any man question God's authority and who is man to question God. Nothing that is created can claim authority over the creator or question the works of the creator. God said He will have mercy on those whom He would want to have mercy; and it is His prerogative.

This, however, does not absolve the decision that one has to necessarily take of confessing by mouth and believing in heart that Lord Jesus Christ is the Son of God and Savior. Jesus said He is the way, the truth and the life and no one can come to the Father but by Him. The scripture also says:

"For God so loved the world, that he gave his only begotten Son, that whosoever believeth in him should not perish, but have everlasting life: (John 3:16). There is an important clause in this verse and it is "whosoever" and this clause should not be ignored. That is to say whosoever believes in Lord Jesus Christ will have everlasting life.

God chose Abraham, Isaac, Jacob as His own people and the nation of Israel as His own nation. He honored David, Solomon and they were chosen by God to fulfill His purposes.

PREDESTINATION | LESLIE JOHN

Jesus chose to be born in the lineage of David and the Scriptures say that the Kingdom through David and Solomon will be established for ever and ever. Lord Jesus Christ will rule for a thousand year period from the throne of David. When Lord Jesus Christ was on this earth He chose disciples according to His choice and not by recommendation by anyone or any procedure like that of elections in political circles.

"For thou art an holy people unto the LORD thy God: the LORD thy God hath chosen thee to be a special people unto himself, above all people that are upon the face of the earth" (Deuteronomy 7:6)

"Who are Israelites; to whom pertaineth the adoption, and the glory, and the covenants, and the giving of the law, and the service of God, and the promises" (Romans 9:4)

Addressing believers at Thessalonica Apostle Paul says:

"Let no man deceive you by any means: for that day shall not come, except there come a falling away first, and that man of sin be revealed, the son of perdition" (2 Thessalonians 2:3)

The Scripture says that Antichrist, the son of perdition, will be revealed first and then there will be falling away first followed by the "Great Tribulation" and Lord Jesus Christ's second coming.

Some professing Christians who do not believe in Lord Jesus Christ as their personal savior might get drifted from

Page 62

the Truth in those days, thus falling prey to apostasy. Such an ones who fall prey to apostasy and trample the efficacy of the blood of Lord Jesus Christ and reject Him as Savior will have severe consequences.

"But we are bound to give thanks alway to God for you, brethren beloved of the Lord, because God hath from the beginning chosen you to salvation through sanctification of the Spirit and belief of the truth" (2 Thessalonians 2:13)

"For if we sin wilfully after that we have received the knowledge of the truth, there remaineth no more sacrifice for sins". (Hebrews 10:26)

Continuing on the same thought Paul says in vs. 13 that we ought to give thanks always to God because God has chosen us from the beginning to salvation through sanctification of the Spirit and belief of the truth. The doctrine of election by grace is surely true. The basis for election to be conformed to the image of Lord Jesus Christ is the good pleasure of God.

"Having predestinated us unto the adoption of children by Jesus Christ to himself, according to the good pleasure of his will" (Ephesians 1:5)

Speaking about the election of Apostles Lord Jesus Christ said "Ye have not chosen me, but I have chosen you, and ordained you, that ye should go and bring forth fruit, and that your fruit should remain: that whatsoever ye shall ask of the Father in my name, he may give it you. These things I command you, that ye love one another. If the world hate you, ye know that it hated me before it hated you. If ye were of the world, the world would love his own: but because ye are not of the world, but I have chosen you out of the world, therefore the world hateth you". (John 15:16-19)

"For by grace are ye saved through faith; and that not of yourselves: it is the gift of God" (Ephesians 2:8)

Grace is the gift of God and we are not saved by ourselves. It is when we exercise faith in Him that we are saved. Salvation cannot be purchased by good works, or silver or Gold but it is only through faith in Lord Jesus Christ as Savior that we are saved.

In His foreknowledge God predestined us to be conformed to the image of His Son but not everyone is saved. It is like an invitation given to many but only few invitees accepted the invitation and others rejected. God does not force anyone to accept Him nor reject Him.

God did not choose any one for destruction; it is man by his choice that he faces his destruction. God's chosen ones will accept Him as Savior. Others have the option of accepting or rejecting Him as Savior. There is no salvation except through Lord Jesus Christ.

"That if thou shalt confess with thy mouth the Lord Jesus, and shalt believe in thine heart that God hath raised him from the dead, thou shalt be saved". (Romans 10:9)

CHAPTER 8 SECURITY OF SALVATION

"But God commendeth his love toward us, in that, while we were yet sinners, Christ died for us". (Romans Ch. 5:8)

While we were enemies to God Christ died for our sake. He loved us and had compassion on us. God is not human to take back the gift that He gives to believer in him. It is by hearing the Word of God that the sinner confesses his sins and trusts in the Lord. He lays his faith in God through Jesus Christ.

It is the Father in heaven, who draws unto himself, those that are to be saved. Such faith comes by hearing the Word of God. He who receives Jesus as his personal savior is secure in God's arms. Holy Spirit leads the believer every day and guides his paths.

Eph. Chapter 2:8-10 show us that this gift of salvation cannot be gained through any amount of works of man. No man can boast that he received salvation by doing good works but good works follow after a man has received salvation.

We are the workmanship of God. Any sin is abominable to God and no sin will go unpaid for while the believer is on this earth.

SALVATION IS THE GIFT OF GOD

The gift of God is so precious that once it is given to a believer God cannot deny His own love toward us, nor can He deny His love toward His One and only Son, Jesus Christ that He takes back that gift from us.

Romans 6:23 is a very familiar verse in the Bible. There is one great gift that God gave unto us through His One and Only Son Jesus Christ and that gift is the salvation and it is the greatest gift of all. Wages are the earnings for the work done by someone. Bible calls the wages of sin is death, but the gift of God is eternal life through Jesus Christ our Lord.

The Father in heaven in His mercy sent His One and Only Son Jesus Christ because He loved us first, even when we were dead in our trespasses and saved us by grace.

Salvation can neither be earned through the works nor can it be purchased for a price. It is the gift of God through Lord Jesus Christ. He paid the price for our sins upon the cross of Calvary. He shed His precious blood for our sake and washed our sins in His blood.

The love of God is so great that He found us in our trespasses and sent His One and Only Son, Jesus Christ for our sake, that whosoever believes in Him shall not perish but will have everlasting life.

If we confess our sins, He is faithful and just to forgive us our sins. He sought us because He loved us first. We received salvation not because we loved Him first, but because He loved us first.

THE CHARGE

There are those who charge that salvation of a believer can be lost if he commits sin in his day-to-day life; but this charge is untenable. Salvation of a believer is secure and eternal.

The work of God rendered through His One and only begotten Son, Lord Jesus Christ in extending His grace toward us is everlasting one. He will not take back the salvation from any recipient on any reason.

We are sealed with the Holy Spirit unto redemption. An important fact that should be borne in mind is that a true believer will not sin but will stand firm in his faith in the Lord.

The Scriptures say that one that commits sin is of the devil and one that is born of God does not commit sin (1 John 3:8-9). Anyone who confesses his sins to God and believes that the Son of God, Lord Jesus Christ, died for him and rose from the dead will have salvation and he will have everlasting life.

No temptation is beyond our capacity of tolerance:

"There hath no temptation taken you but such as is common to man: but God is faithful, who will not suffer you to be tempted above that ye are able; but will with the temptation also make a way to escape, that ye may be able to bear it" (1 Corinthians 10:13)

No temptation has ever over taken any believer that he could not find an alternative way to escape from such temptation. God provides alternative way so that the believer may not fall into sin and perish. In spite of such provision available, if believer commits sins he will receive chastisement from God and suffers in this world.

Because he would not be working for the Lord he would lose his rewards also. But salvation is never lost because believer is sealed with the Holy Spirit. It is the gift of God and it is a firm promise from God that he will uphold us and no one can pluck us from out his hand. God will not break His promises.

THE LOVE OF GOD

Apostle Paul says in Romans 8:33-39 that no one can separate us from the love of God. Lord Jesus ascended into heaven after forty days of his resurrection from the dead and he is seated on the right hand of the Majesty. He is pleading with the Father on behalf of us who have salvation Him.

The fact that our Lord Jesus is interceding on behalf of us with the Father in heaven without ceasing is another reason to believe that believer is secure and his salvation is secure. Otherwise, it would mean that the intercession of the only begotten Son, Jesus Christ, on behalf of us is in vain and has no effect.

The Holy Spirit guides and convicts the believer of his failings every moment. The feign thoughts that God, the Father in heaven, can deny the intercession Jesus Christ are too presumptuous to be taken as true. The salvation given to a believer as a merciful gift by His grace will not be taken back.

Every believer should keep in mind that there are rewards for him for the works he does for God after receiving salvation. The rewards are given at the "Judgment seat of Christ" (which is also known as "Bema Seat of Christ") in the mid-air.

The believer, who has truly tasted that love from God, cannot think of falling into sin again and again to repent repeatedly. It would mean crucifying Lord Jesus afresh repeatedly and putting Him to open shame.

Hebrews 6:4-6 reminds us of this fact that a believer, who received the gift of salvation will not think of falling into sin every day to seek refuge under the provisions in the Scriptures about security of the salvation. He would rather lead a holy life pleasing unto the Lord.

GOD HAS CHOSEN US

Speaking to His disciples, Jesus said that He would no longer call them as 'servants', but would call them as friends. The disciples did not become the disciples of Jesus by their own choice, but it was Jesus, who chose them as His disciples. He ordained that they should go and bring forth fruit unto the Lord.

The words of Lord Jesus Christ help us to understand that the salvation of a believer in Christ is secure and eternal. Jesus' own words as recorded in John 10:29 are beyond doubt that He holds us firm in his fold.

"My Father, which gave them me, is greater than all; and no man is able to pluck them out of my Father's hand". (John 10:29)

"Herein is love, not that we loved God, but that he loved us, and sent his Son to be the propitiation for our sins. (1 John 4:10)

Jesus also promised His disciples that whatever they ask of the Father in heaven in His name, He would give unto them. They did not belong to this world, and because they did not belong to the world, Jesus chose them. (John 15:16) Whoever receives Jesus as his/her personal Savior, to them God gave power to become the sons of God (John 1:12).

Jesus gives eternal life to all those, who believe in Him, so that they shall never perish, nor can anyone pluck the believer out of His hand. The Word of God is so clear here in John 10:28-30 that no one can pluck a believer out of His hand.

"And I give unto them eternal life; and they shall never perish, neither shall any man pluck them out of my hand. My Father, which gave them me, is greater than all; and no man is able to pluck them out of my Father's hand. I and my Father are one". (John 10:28-30)

A believer can trust in the words of Lord Jesus Christ, just as Apostle Paul affirmed in Romans 8:38-39, that neither anyone or any act, or any power, can separate us from the love of God, because we are in Christ Jesus and let us, therefore, give thanks unto the Father in heaven, just as Apostle Paul asked us to do in Colossians 1:1-13.

God made us partakers in the inheritance of the saints in light and delivered from the power of darkness in order to translate us into the Kingdom of His One and Only Son, Jesus Christ. We believe in the gospel of Jesus Christ and about the eternal life that Jesus promised to us and we are sealed with the Holy Spirit of promise.

We are purchased possession of our God so that we may be unto him the praise of his glory. We should bear in mind the hope of our calling, and know "what the riches of the glory of his inheritance in the saints" (Eph.1:13-18)

THE SEVERITY OF JUDGMENT

The writer of Hebrews warns about the severity of the judgment of God that falls on those that sin willfully trampling down the sacrifice of our Only High Priest, Lord Jesus Christ and apostatizes. Hebrews 10:26-31 deal with this dilemma that Christians attribute to salvation being lost in case a believer in Christ commits sin. These verses show us the importance of realizing who the Son of God is, and the results deliberate denial and renunciation of the faith in Christ fetches.

In the Old Testament the greatest of all punishments was awarded to deliberate denial of the Word of the LORD. "Because he hath despised the word of the LORD, and hath broken his commandment, that soul shall utterly be cut off; his iniquity shall be upon him" (Numbers 15:31). Such punishment is awarded to those, who deliberately renounce the Son of God and tread Him down under foot.

The recognition of the efficacy of the blood of Jesus Christ and his High Priest-hood stands out to be the dominant demand from anyone in the world. One that is saved will never renounce Lord Jesus Christ and the efficacy of His blood shed upon the cross of Calvary.

It is, therefore, beyond doubt that only unbeliever can tread down the Son of God under his feet and face the serious consequences of being thrown into the 'lake of fire'. The believer in Christ is secure eternally inasmuch as his belief in Lord Jesus Christ as his personal savior involves inseparable union with Christ and the death to sin (Romans 6:6-8).

If any believer in Christ strives to trample upon the Son of God and denies Him, God will make him kneel down on his feet with enough chastisement, and acknowledge that Jesus is the Lord, and reaffirm that He is the Savior

CHAPTER 9

SALVATION FOR EVERY ONE

"Ho, every one that thirsteth, come ye to the waters, and he that hath no money; come ye, buy, and eat; yea, come, buy wine and milk without money and without price". (Isaiah 55:1)

Isaiah Chapter 53 had prophecy about the crucifixion of Jesus Christ and Isaiah Chapter 54 has blessings and protection to the Children of Israel. In Isaiah Chapter 55 there is a call for every one which includes you and me. The calling is for everyone who thirsts to come to the waters. This is a call for salvation which is available free of cost but there should be thirst to have it.

he salvation is to be sought for. There needs to be desire to have it and there needs to be desire to accept it free of cost. God does not want any of our works or money to be used for receiving that which is given free of cost and the price for which is already paid for. The price is paid for by Jesus Christ on the cross.

Matthew Chapter 13:44-46 describe the desire one has to have to receive the kingdom of heaven, which is like a treasure hidden in a field.

The parable says that when a man finds the field that has treasure in it, he goes and sells his entire assets and buys that field. Also it is compared to an expensive pearl that a man buys by selling his entire assets. Luke Chapter 14:33 says that, whoever does not forsake all that he has, cannot become the disciple of Jesus Christ. Salvation is so precious but it cannot be bought with silver and gold.

The Lord says that his thoughts are higher than ours and his ways are higher than ours. His thoughts are not our thoughts and his ways are not our ways. "For my thoughts are not your thoughts, neither are your ways my ways, saith the LORD" (Isaiah 55:8)

The wise man says in Proverbs that there is a way that seems good for a man but it leads to destruction. "There is a way which seemeth right unto a man, but the end thereof are the ways of death". (Proverbs 14:12) When God interferes in the lives of believers it is for chastening them and to place them in a secure place.

The Lord says that just as the rain and snow come down from heaven and water the ground and they do not return but make the earth to bring forth plants and trees that benefit the sower, so is his word that goes forth out of his mouth. It shall not return void but it shall accomplish that which the Lord pleases and it prospers to fulfill the purpose for which it was sent out.

"So shall my word be that goeth forth out of my mouth: it shall not return unto me void, but it shall accomplish that which I please, and it shall prosper in the thing whereto I sent it". (Isaiah 55:11)

There is an assurance for the one who believes in the Lord that he shall go out with joy and be led with peace. There will be heavenly blessings showered on him. (Isaiah 55:12-13). But it should not be misunderstood that the life of a believer on this earth will be like bed of roses. Surely we will have our rewards in heaven.

Jesus has forgiven many with grave sins when they sought him. In Jesus alone is salvation. Seek him while he may be found. Jesus said to the woman of Samaria that he will give living water. (John 4:10) Today is the day of Salvation. It is your choice. Jesus Christ, who bore our sins and died for our sake, is resurrected and He is living God. He will come soon to receive the saved ones to be with Him eternally. God has his own ways of gaining men for himself.

My message is a request that you may please accept Jesus Christ as your personal Savior, and as your Lord, so that you may have everlasting life just as I have gained peace through Him.

www.ingramcontent.com/pod-product-compliance
Lightning Source LLC
Chambersburg PA
CBHW021141020426
42331CB00005B/857